PYTHON FOR BLOCKCHAIN DEVELOPMENT 2024

Building Smart Contracts with Python Programming for Beginners

BY

BETH KELVIN C.

Table of Contents

INTRODUCTION TO PYTHON AND BLOCKCHAIN

<u>**Overview of Python Programming Language:**</u>

1. **Python's Simplicity and Readability**

• Python is famed for its simplicity and readability, making it an ideal programming language for both newcomers and educated inventors. Its clean syntax and use of indentation for block structures contribute to law readability.

2. **Versatility and Ease of Learning**

• Python's versatility allows inventors to work on a wide range of operations, from web development and data analysis to artificial intelligence and scientific computing. The language's straightforward syntax and expansive attestation make it easy for beginners to grasp.

3. Rich Standard Library

• Python comes with a rich standard library, offering modules and packages for colorful tasks, reducing the need for external dependences. This point enhances development effectiveness and simplifies common programming tasks.

4. Community Support and coffers

• Python boasts a vibrant and probative community. Inventors can pierce a wealth of coffers, including forums, attestation, and online tutorials. The cooperative nature of the

Python community contributes to its continual growth and enhancement.

5. Comity and Integration

• Python is compatible with colorful platforms and operating systems, fostering cross-platform development. Also, it supports flawless integration with other languages, easing the objectification of Python law into being systems.

6. Object- acquainted Programming (OOP)

• Python is an object- acquainted programming language, promoting law association and modularity.

This paradigm allows inventors to structure their law using objects and classes, leading to further justifiable and scalable operations.

7. Expansive Libraries and fabrics

- Python's expansive ecosystem includes libraries and fabrics that streamline development in colorful disciplines. Notable exemplifications include Django for web development, NumPy for scientific computing, and Tensor Flow for machine literacy.

Introduction to Blockchain Technology:

1. Decentralization and Distributed Ledger

Blockchain is a decentralized and distributed tally technology that enables the secure and transparent recording of deals across a network of computers. Each party in the network has a dupe of the entire tally, enhancing translucency and adaptability.

2. Invariability and Cryptography

- Blockchain achieves invariability through cryptographic mincing. Each block in the chain contains a hash of the former block, creating a secure and tamper-resistant sequence.

Once a block is added, altering any former block would bear changing all posterior blocks, making the system largely secure.

3. Consensus Mechanisms

Consensus mechanisms, like Proof of Work (POW) and evidence of Stake (PoS), ensure agreement among actors on the validity of deals. POW requires actors to break complex fine problems, while PoS relies on actors holding a stake in the cryptocurrency.

4. Smart Contracts

Smart contracts are tone-executing contracts with the terms of the agreement directly written into law.

They automate and apply the prosecution of contractual clauses, barring the need for interposers. Ethereum is a popular blockchain platform for enforcing smart contracts.

5. Cryptocurrencies and Commemoratives

Numerous blockchains host their native cryptocurrencies (e.g., Bitcoin, Ether). Also, commemoratives, representing means or mileage, can be created on blockchain platforms.

These digital means can be transferred securely and transparently on the blockchain.

6. Use Cases beyond Cryptocurrencies

While cryptocurrencies were the original use case, blockchain technology has expanded to colorful diligence. Operations include force chain operations, healthcare data exchange, advancing systems, and decentralized finance (DeFi).

7. Challenges and Scalability

Despite its eventuality, blockchain faces challenges, including scalability issues, high energy consumption (in POW systems), and nonsupervisory enterprises. Ongoing exploration and development aim to address these challenges and enhance the connection of blockchain technology.

8. Permissioned and Permissionless Blockchains

Blockchain networks can be permission (confined access) or permissionless (open to anyone). Permissioned blockchains are frequently employed in enterprise settings, furnishing controlled access to a destined group of actors.

9. Blockchain Development Platforms

Inventors can produce decentralized operations (DApps) and smart contracts using colorful blockchain development platforms. Ethereum, Binance Smart Chain, and Hyperledger are exemplifications of platforms offering tools and fabrics for blockchain development.

10. Arising Trends

Arising trends in blockchain technology include the rise of non-fungible commemoratives (NFTs), which represent unique digital means, and the discourse of blockchain in sustainability sweats, aiming to address the environmental impact of certain agreement mechanisms.

In summary, Python's simplicity, versatility, and expansive ecosystem make it an important language for blockchain development.

Understanding blockchain technology, with its decentralized and transparent nature, opens doors to a wide array of operations across diligence.

As the fields of Python and blockchain continue to evolve, the community between them is likely to drive invention in decentralized systems and operations.

UNDERSTANDING SMART CONTRACTS

Definition and Principles of Smart Contracts:

1. Definition:

A smart contract is a tone- executing contract with the terms of the agreement directly written into law. It operates on a blockchain, where the law executes automatically when predefined conditions are met. Smart contracts aim to automate and apply the prosecution of contractual agreements without the need for interposers.

2. Law as Law

• The principle behind smart contracts is frequently expressed as" law is law." Once stationed on the blockchain, the law governing the smart contract becomes the definitive authority, and its prosecution is irrevocable. This principle enhances trust among parties, as the terms are transparent, empirical, and tone- administering.

3. Decentralization

Smart contracts operate in a decentralized manner, running on a distributed network of bumps that validate and execute deals. This decentralized nature ensures that there's no single point of failure and no need for a trusted conciliator to oversee the contract's prosecution.

4. Invariability

Once stationed on the blockchain, smart contracts are inflexible, meaning their law cannot be altered or tampered with.

Invariability ensures that the terms of the contract remain unchanged and that the history of contract prosecution is transparent and empirical.

5. Tokenization

Smart contracts frequently involve the use of commemoratives, representing digital means or mileage within the ecosystem. These commemoratives can be transferred securely and transparently between parties as part of the contract's prosecution.

6. Tentative prosecution

Smart contracts execute automatically when predefined conditions are met. These conditions, decoded in the contract's law, could include time-grounded triggers, specific events on the blockchain, or input from external systems through oracles.

Benefits of Smart Contracts

1. Trust and translucency

Smart contracts enhance trust between parties by furnishing translucency into the terms and prosecution of agreements. All actors can check the law and corroborate the contract's state on the blockchain.

2. Reduced interposers and Costs

By automating contract prosecution, smart contracts exclude the need for interposers, similar as banks or legal realities, reducing associated costs. This effectiveness can lead to briskly deals and lower freights.

3. Invariability and Security

The invariability of smart contracts ensures that formerly stationed, their law cannot be altered, furnishing a high position of security against tampering or fraud. This point is particularly pivotal in fiscal and legal operations.

4. Automated prosecution and effectiveness

Smart contracts execute automatically when conditions are met, reducing the need for homemade intervention. This robotization not only increases effectiveness but also reduces the liability of crimes associated with homemade processes.

5. Global Availability

Smart contracts operate on blockchain networks that are accessible encyclopedically. This opens up openings forcross-border deals and collaborations without the need for interposers handling transnational aspects of agreements.

6. Tokenization and Programmable Assets

Smart contracts frequently involve the use of commemoratives, enabling the representation of colorful means (e.g., digital currencies, real estate) and programmable functionalities within the blockchain ecosystem.

7. Decentralization and Adaptability

The decentralized nature of smart contracts ensures that they operate on a network of bumps, making them flexible to single points of failure.

This characteristic enhances trustability and robustness.

Use Cases of Smart Contracts

1. Financial Services

Automated prosecution of fiscal agreements, similar as loans, insurance, and decentralized finance (DeFi) operations, where smart contracts grease lending, borrowing, and trading.

2. Supply Chain Management

Smart contracts can automate and corroborate force chain processes, icing translucency and traceability of goods from product to delivery.

3. Real Estate

Easing transparent and effective real estate deals by automating processes similar as property transfers, escrow, and rental agreements.

4. Legal Contracts and Agreements

Executing and administering legal contracts, including agreements related to intellectual property, employment, and any contractual arrangement where predefined conditions can be decoded.

5. Healthcare Data Management

Icing secure and sequestration- conserving operation of healthcare data, allowing for transparent and auditable sharing of case records among sanctioned parties.

6. Voting Systems

Enforcing secure and transparent voting systems that can exclude fraud and enhance the integrity of election processes.

7. Gaming and Entertainment

Enabling the creation of decentralized operations (DApps) for gaming and entertainment diligence, where smart contracts govern in- game deals, digital asset power, and prices distribution.

8. Cross-Border Payments

Easing transnational deals with reduced freights and briskly agreement times, especially salutary in scripts where traditional banking systems might be slow or precious.

9. Token Immolations (ICOs, STOs)

Conducting token deals, similar as original Coin Immolations (ICOs) and Security Token Offerings (STOs), where smart contracts govern the allocation, distribution, and compliance aspects of commemoratives.

10. Intellectual Property and Royalties

Managing intellectual property rights and automating kingliness payments for content generators, musicians, pens, and artists through smart contracts. Understanding smart contracts involves feting their foundational principles, similar as decentralization, invariability, and tentative prosecution.

The benefits of trust, translucency, effectiveness, and cost reduction make smart contracts applicable in a wide range of diligence, revolutionizing traditional processes and paving the way for innovative decentralized operations.

PYTHON BASICS FOR BLOCKCHAIN

<u>**Python Syntax and Fundamentals:**</u>

1. Variables and Data Types

• Python uses dynamic typing, allowing variables to change their type during runtime. Common data types include integers, floats, strings, lists, tuples, and wordbooks. Variables are assigned using the" = "driver.

Illustration x = 5 name = "John"

2. Control Flow

Python supports tentative statements (if, Elif, differently) and circles (for, while). Indentation is pivotal for law blocks.

Illustration if x> 0 print (" Positive")   additional print
("Non-positive")

3. Functions

Functions are defined using the def keyword. Arguments can be passed, and functions can return values.

Example

*Def square (num) return num ** 2*

Result = Square (3)

4. Lists and wordbooks

Lists are ordered collections, and wordbooks are crucial- value dyads. They're variable and protean.

Illustration

My list= (1, 2, 3)

My dict = {' name" Alice',' age' 30}

5. Classes and Objects

Python supports object- acquainted programming. Classes are arrangements for objects.

Example

Class Dog

Def, init, (tone, name)

self.name = name

My dog= Canine (" Buddy")

6. Exception Handling

Python provides try, except, and eventually blocks for handling exceptions.

Illustration

Pass

Result = 10/ 0

Except ZeroDivisionError

Print (" Cannot divide by zero")

7. Train Handling

Reading from and writing to lines is straightforward in Python.

Illustration (Reading)

With open ('file.txt',' r') as train

Content = file.read ()

Illustration (Writing)

With open ('new_file.txt',' w') as train

file.write (' Hello, World!')

<u>Setting up a Python Development Environment for Blockchain</u>

1. Python Installation

Install Python from the sanctioned website (https//www.python.org/). Insure that you check the option to add Python to the system PATH during installation.

2. Virtual surroundings

Use virtual surroundings to insulate design dependences. Produce a virtual terrain using

Python- m venv myenv

Spark the virtual terrain

On Windows

Myenv Scripts spark

On macOS Linux

Source myenv/ caddy/ spark

3. Package Management with pip

Pip is Python's package installer. Use it to install packages like web3 for interacting with the Ethereum blockchain

Pip install web3

4. Integrated Development Environment (IDE)

Choose an IDE for Python development. Popular choices include VSCode, PyCharm, and Jupyter Scrapbooks.

These IDEs offer features like law completion, debugging, and design operation.

5. Blockchain Development Libraries

Install libraries for blockchain development. For Ethereum, you can use libraries like web3.py. Install it using

Pip install web3

6. Version Control

Use interpretation control systems like Git to manage law changes. Host your law on platforms like GitHub for collaboration.

Initialize a Git depository git init

Produce a new depository on GitHub, also push your law

Git remote add origin

Git add.

Git commit- m" original commit"

Git drive- u origin master

7. Blockchain Node

Depending on the blockchain you are working with, you might need to set up an original knot for testing. For Ethereum, tools like Ganache give an original blockchain terrain.

8. Testing Blockchain relations

Use testnets (test networks) to emplace and test smart contracts without using real crypto currency. Ethereum has testnets like Ropsten and Rinkeby.

Setting up a Python development terrain for blockchain involves creating a solid foundation with Python, essential libraries, and tools specific to the blockchain platform you are working with. Whether it's Ethereum, Bitcoin, or another blockchain, Python's versatility and well-configured terrain will streamline your development process.

BLOCKCHAIN FUNDAMENTALS

Decentralization, Consensus Mechanisms, and Distributed Ledger Technology:

1. Decentralization

• Decentralization is an abecedarian principle of blockchain technology. In a decentralized system, there's no central authority or central controlling the network. Rather, multiple bumps (computers) share in the confirmation and verification of deals, leading to increased trust, security, and adaptability.

2. Consensus Mechanisms

• Consensus mechanisms are protocols that insure all bumps in a blockchain network agree on the validity of deals. Common agreement mechanisms include

Evidence of Work (POW): Bumps (miners) break complex fine problems to validate deals and add blocks to the blockchain. Bitcoin uses POW.

Evidence of Stake (PoS): Validators are chosen grounded on the quantum of cryptocurrency they hold. PoS aims to reduce energy consumption compared to POW.

Delegated Proof of Stake (DPoS): Token holders bounce for a limited number of delegates who validate deals. DPoS enhances scalability.

Evidence of Authority (PoA): Validators are known realities, generally chosen grounded on character or authority. PoA is common in private or institute blockchains.

3. Distributed Ledger Technology (DLT)

• A distributed tally is a database that's distributed and accompanied across multiple bumps in a network. Each party has a dupe of the tally, and any changes are reflected across the entire network. Blockchain is a specific type of DLT, characterized by its use of blocks and cryptographic mincing to secure deals.

4. Invariability

• Invariability is a crucial specific of distributed tally technology. Once a block is added to the blockchain, it cannot be altered or removed. This ensures the integrity and translucency of the sale history.

5. Cryptography

• Cryptography plays a pivotal part in securing deals and maintaining the sequestration of actors.

Public and private keys are used to subscribe and corroborate deals, furnishing a secure and tamper-resistant terrain.

6. Smart Contracts

• Smart contracts are tone- executing contracts with the terms directly written into law. They automate and apply the prosecution of agreements, barring the need for interposers.

Ethereum is a popular blockchain platform for enforcing smart contracts.

7. Bumps and Mining

• Bumps are computers that share in the blockchain network. Mining bumps (in POW systems) validate deals and add blocks to the chain. Full bumps store the entire blockchain and validate deals without sharing in the mining process.

• Blockchain allows the creation of commemoratives, representing digital means or mileage within the ecosystem. These commemoratives can be transferred securely and transparently on the blockchain, enabling colorful use cases like cryptocurrencies, decentralized finance (DeFi), and non-fungible commemoratives (NFTs).

Public vs Private Blockchains

1. Public Blockchains

Availability: Public blockchains are open to anyone, allowing anyone to share, validate deals, and join the network.

Decentralization: Public blockchains are generally more decentralized, involving a large number of bumps encyclopedically.

Exemplifications: Bitcoin and Ethereum are exemplifications of public blockchains.

2. Private Blockchains

Permissioned Access: Private Blockchains circumscribe access, taking authorization to join. Actors are frequently known realities or associations.

Control: Private Blockchains offer further control to actors, making them suitable for business colleges or enterprises.

Exemplifications: Hyperledger Fabric and R3 Corda are exemplifications of private or institute blockchains.

3. Consortium Blockchains

* **Intermediate Level:** Consortium blockchains are semi-decentralized. They involve a group of

known realities or associations that inclusively control the network.

• **Use Cases:** Suitable for diligence where collaboration is needed but complete decentralization isn't practical, similar as force chain operation.

4. Mongrel Blockchains

• **Combination of Features:** mongrel blockchains combine rudiments of both public and private blockchains to influence the benefits of both models.

• **Inflexibility:** This model provides inflexibility, allowing certain deals to be public while others remain private.

• **Public:** Public blockchains may face scalability challenges due to a large number of actors and global agreement mechanisms.

• **Private:** Private Blockchains can offer better scalability and performance since they involve a known and frequently lower set of actors. Understanding blockchain fundamentals involves grasping the generalities of decentralization, agreement mechanisms, and distributed tally technology. Also, feting the differences between public and private blockchains is pivotal for determining the felicity of a blockchain result for a particular use case or assiduity.

PREFACE TO SOLIDITY

Overview of Solidity Programming Language

1. Purpose and Use

Solidity is a high- position programming language designed for developing smart contracts that run on the Ethereum Virtual Machine (EVM). It's a statically- compartmented language told by JavaScript, Python, and C. reliability facilitates the creation of tone- executing contracts with predefined conditions.

2. Ethereum Smart Contracts

Solidity is primarily used for writing Ethereum smart contracts. Smart contracts are tone-executing programs with the terms of the contract directly written into law. They automatically

apply and execute contract rules on the Ethereum
blockchain.

3. Syntax and Structure

• Reliability syntax is analogous to that of
JavaScript. It includes generalities similar as
functions, variables, control structures, and
object- acquainted features like heritage and
polymorphism. Reliability source law lines
generally have a. sol extension. /illustration
reliability Contract

Contract SimpleStorage {

Uint256 storedData;

Function set (uint256 x) public {

StoredData = x;

Function get () public view returns (uint256) {

Return storedData;

4. Data Types

• Reliability supports colorful data types, including integers, booleans, strings, arrays, and more. It also includes special types for dealing with Ethereum-specific generalities like addresses and the contract itself.

/ Example Data Types

Uint256 public number;

Address public proprietor;

String public communication;

5. Functions and Modifiers

• Reliability contracts correspond of functions that define the behavior of the smart contract. Modifiers are used to modify the geste of functions. For illustration, the view modifier indicates that a function doesn't modify the contract's state.

// Example Function and Modifier

Function set Message (string memory _message) public {

Require (msg.sender == owner, "Only owner can set

message");

Message = _message;

}

Modifier onlyOwner () {

Require (msg.sender == owner, "Only owner can call

this function");

_;

}

6. Events

Reliability contracts can emit events, which are logs of specific circumstances within the contract. Events can be used to notify external operations about state changes.

// Example Event

Event MessageSet (string message, address indexed setter);

Function setMessage (string memory _message) public onlyOwner {

Message = _message;

Emit MessageSet (_message, msg.sender);

}

7. **Inheritance:**

• Reliability supports heritage, allowing contracts to inherit parcels and styles from other contracts. This promotes law reusability and modularity.

```
// Example Inheritance
Contract Ownable {
Address public owner;
Modifier onlyOwner () {
Require (msg.sender == owner, "Only owner can
call this function");
_;
}
}

Contract SimpleStorage is Ownable {
Uint256 storedData;

Function set (uint256 x) public onlyOwner {
StoredData = x;
}
}
```

Writing and Deploying a Simple Smart Contract in Solidity:

1. Writing a Simple Smart Contract:

- Let's produce a simple reliability smart contract named Simple Storage. This contract allows a proprietor to set and recoup a stored integer value.

// SimpleStorage.sol

// SPDX-License-Identifier: MIT

Pragma solidity ^0.8.0;

Contract SimpleStorage {

Uint256 storedData;

Function set (uint256 x) public {

StoredData = x;

}

Function get () public view returns (uint256) {

Return storedData;

}

}

2. Compiling the Contract:

• Use a reliability compiler, similar as solc, to collect the smart contract. You can also use online reliability development surroundings that give compendium features.

Solc SimpleStorage.sol --bin --abi --optimize -o. /output

3. **Deploying the Contract:**

• To emplace the contract, you need an Ethereum portmanteau and a deployment tool like Remix or Truffle. In this illustration, we'll use Remix, a web-grounded IDE for Ethereum smart contract development.

• Copy the collected bytecode and ABI (operation double Interface) from the compendium affair.

4. **Deploying on Remix:**

• Open Remix (https//remix.ethereum.org/), produce a new train, bury your reliability law, and collect it using the reliability compiler plugin.

• Go to the" Emplace & Run Deals" tab, elect the terrain (JavaScript VM, fitted Web3, or a custom Ethereum knot), and click" Emplace" to emplace the contract.

5. Interacting with the Contract:

• Once stationed, you can interact with the contract using the handed functions.

For illustration, you can call the set function to set a value and also call the progeny function to recoup it.

• You can view sale details and contract state changes on the Ethereum blockchain discoverer.

Solidity serves as the ground between inventors and the Ethereum blockchain, enabling the creation of decentralized operations and smart contracts. Writing and planting a simple smart contract in reliability provides hands- on experience in using blockchain technology for programmable and transparent agreements.

BUILDING SMART CONTRACTS WITH PYTHON

<u>**Integrating Python with Smart Contract**</u>

<u>**Development:**</u>

1. Web3.py Library

•Web3.py is a popular Python library that enables commerce with Ethereum- grounded smart contracts. It provides a Pythonic interface to interact with the Ethereum blockchain, allowing inventors to emplace and interact with smart contracts using Python.

2. Installation

   • InstallWeb3.py using pip

3. Linking to a Blockchain:

To link to an Ethereum node, use Web3.py. Either a local node or a distant node can be connected to.

From web3 import Web3 # Connect to a local Ethereum node w3 = Web3 (Web3.HTTPProvider ('http://localhost:8545')) # Check connection status if w3.isConnected (): print ("Connected to Ethereum node") else: print ("Connection failed")

4. Deploying a Smart Contract:

• To add a smart contract to the Ethereum blockchain, use Web3.py. This entails putting the Solidity code together, making a contract object, and then utilizing a transaction to deploy it.

```python
From web3 import Web3

From solcx import compile_source


# Solidity source code

contract_source = """

Pragma solidity ^0.8.0;


Contract SimpleStorage {

Uint256 storedData;


Function set (uint256 x) public {

StoredData = x;

}


Function get () public view returns (uint256) {

Return storedData;

}

}

"""
```

```python
# Compile Solidity source code
compiled_contract = compile source (contract source)
# Get contract interface and bytecode
Contract interface = compiled_contract ['<stdin>:
SimpleStorage']
Bytecode = contract interface ['bin']
Abi = contract interface ['abi']
# Deploy the contract
w3.eth.default_account = w3.eth.accounts [0]
SimpleStorage = w3.eth.contract (abi=abi,
bytecode=bytecode)
tx_hash = SimpleStorage. Constructor ().transact ()
tx_receipt = w3.eth.waitForTransactionReceipt
(tx_hash)
# Get the deployed contract address
Contract address = tx_receipt ['contractAddress']
Print (f"Contract deployed at: {contract address}")
```

5. Interacting with the Smart Contract:

- To build a contract object in Python, use the address and ABI of the deployed contract. The features of the smart contract may then be accessed and utilized using this object.

 # create contract object

Simple storage = w3.eth.contract (address=contract address, abi=abi)

 # Interact with the smart contract

simple_storage.functions.set (42).transact ()

stored_value = simple_storage.functions.get ().call ()

Print (f"Stored value: {stored_value}")

<u>Creating a Basic Python-Based Smart Contract:</u>

1. **Python Smart Contract using Brownie:**

   - Brownie is an Ethereum smart contract development framework that streamlines the process of developing, testing, and deploying smart contracts. It offers a Pythonic interface for the construction of smart contracts and is developed in the language.

2. **Installation:**

a. Install Brownie using pip:

Pip install eth-brownie

3. **Writing a Basic Smart Contract:**

• Make a new Brownie project and use Python to construct a basic smart contract. An illustration of a basic storage smart contract is shown below.

SimpleStorage.sol pragma solidity ^0.8.0; contract
SimpleStorage {uint256 storedData; function set
(uint256 x) public {storedData = x ;} function get ()
public view returns (uint256) {return storedData ;}}

4. Planting and Interacting with the Smart Contract

- *Use Brownie to emplace and interact with the smart contract. deploy.py*

From elf import SimpleStorage, accounts, network

Def main ()

Emplace the smart contract =

SimpleStorage.deploy ({' from' accounts (0)})

Interact with the smart contract.

Set (42, {' from' accounts (0)})

stored_value = simple_storage. Get ({' from' accounts (0)})

Print (f" Stored value {stored_value}")

5. Running the Deployment Script

- Run the deployment script using the elf press

Replace with the asked Ethereum network (e.g., mainnet, rinkeby, or development).

Python provides accessible tools and libraries for interacting with smart contracts, making it accessible for inventors to make decentralized operations on the Ethereum blockchain.

Whether usingWeb3.py for homemade commerce or elf for a further streamlined development experience, Python's simplicity and expressiveness make it a suitable language for smart contract development.

SMART CONTRACT SECURITY

Smart contract security is pivotal in the blockchain ecosystem to cover digital means, maintain the integrity of decentralized operations, and help vulnerabilities that can be exploited by vicious actors.

Then, we'll explore common security vulnerabilities in smart contracts and stylish practices to enhance their security.

Common Security Vulnerabilities in Smart Contracts

1. Reentrancy Attacks

• Reentrancy occurs when an external contract makes a message to the calling contract before completing its prosecution. This can lead to unanticipated geste, allowing vicious contracts to constantly call back and drain finances.

2. Integer Overflow/ Underflow

• Integer overflow and underflow vulnerabilities arise when fine operations affect in values outside the anticipated range for integer variables. Bushwhackers can manipulate these vulnerabilities to their advantage, causing unanticipated issues.

3. Unbounded External Calls

• External calls to other contracts can introduce security pitfalls. Failing to check the return value of an external call can lead to unanticipated geste, and vicious contracts may exploit this to execute uninvited law.

4. Denial of Service (DoS)

• Smart contracts may be vulnerable to DoS attacks where a bushwhacker exploits loopholes in the contract sense to consume inordinate gas, leading to the prostration of coffers and rendering the contract unworkable.

5. Front- Running

• Front- running occurs when a bushwhacker exploits the order of deals to gain an advantage. This can be problematic in fiscal operations, allowing bushwhackers to manipulate the order of deals for particular gain.

6. Timestamp Dependence

• counting on timestamp values in smart contracts can be parlous, as miners have some control over the block timestamp.

Bushwhackers may manipulate timestamps to impact contract geste.

Best Practices for Securing Smart Contract Code

1. **Use Safe Math Libraries**

• use safe calculation libraries to help integer overflow and underflow vulnerabilities. Libraries like Open Zeppelin's Safe Math give secure computation operations.

2. **Check- goods- relations Pattern**

• Follow the" Check- goods- relations" pattern, where state changes are performed after icing that external calls have completed successfully. This helps help reentrancy attacks.

3. Avoid External Calls in the Constructor

• Avoid making external calls in the constructor, as this can introduce security pitfalls. External calls should be made with caution, and their return values should always be checked.

4. Gas Limit Considerations

• Be aware of gas limits in Ethereum deals. Insure that functions are designed to operate within reasonable gas limits to avoid implicit DoS attacks.

5. Use Reentrancy Guard

• apply reentrancy protection using constructs like the ReentrancyGuard from OpenZeppelin. This can help help reentrancy attacks by furnishing a modifier that ensures only one external call is in progress at a time.

6. Use the rearmost reliability interpretation

• Keep the reliability compiler up to date with the rearmost interpretation to work security advancements and bug fixes. Regularly check for updates and resettle contracts to newer compiler performances as demanded.

7. Code Audits and Testing

• Conduct thorough law checkups and testing, both manually and using automated tools. Peer reviews and external checkups by security experts can help identify implicit vulnerabilities and ameliorate law quality.

8. Avoid Timestamp Dependence

• Minimize reliance on block timestamps, as they can be manipulated by miners. Consider using indispensable styles or external timestamp oracles for critical time-dependent operations.

9. Limit the Use of External Calls

• Minimize the use of external calls whenever possible. However, insure that they're made to trusted contracts and validate return values to avoid unanticipated geste, if external calls are necessary.

10. Apply Access Controls

• Use access control mechanisms to circumscribe warrants and define who can execute specific functions in the smart contract. Use modifiers like" onlyOwner" to limit access to critical functions.

11. Nonstop Monitoring

• Cover the blockchain for unusual conditioning and deals related to the smart contract. Apply mechanisms for nonstop monitoring and waking to respond snappily to implicit security incidents.

12.Educate druggies

• give clear attestation and educate druggies about the proper use of your smart contract. Easily communicate implicit pitfalls, limitations, and security stylish practices to druggies.

By following these stylish practices and remaining watchful in addressing arising security enterprises, inventors can significantly enhance the security of their smart contracts.

Nonstop enhancement, collaboration, and a visionary approach to security are essential rudiments in erecting robust and secure decentralized operations.

INTERACTING WITH SMART CONTRACTS

Interacting with smart contracts is a pivotal aspect of developing decentralized operations (DApps) and blockchain- grounded systems.

In this environment, we'll explore how to call and interact with smart contracts using Python, fastening on different styles of commerce.

Calling and Interacting with Smart Contracts using Python

1. Web3.py Library

•Web3.py is an extensively used Python library for interacting with Ethereum- grounded smart contracts. It provides an accessible interface to connect to an Ethereum knot, emplace smart contracts, and interact with their functions.

2. Installation

- InstallWeb3.py using pip

Pip install web3

3. Combining to an Ethereum Node

- Connect to an Ethereum knot usingWeb3.py. You can connect to an original knot or a remote knot.

From web3 import Web3

Connect to a original Ethereum knot

w3 = Web3 (Web3.HTTPProvider (' http//

localhost8545'))

Check connection status

ifw3.isConnected ()

Print (" Connected to Ethereum knot")

Additional

Print (" Connection failed")

4. **Creating a Contract Object**

• Use the smart contract's ABI (operation double Interface) and address to produce a contract object. The ABI is a JSON representation of the contract's functions and parameters.

ABI and address from contract _abi = [...]

contract_address= "0x123abc."

Produce contract object

Contract = w3.eth.contract (address = contract_address,

abi = contract_abi)

5. Calling Contract Functions:

• Interact with the smart contract by calling its functions. Specify the sender's address and gas parameters.

Illustration Call a read-only function

Result = contract.functions.get (). Call ()

Print (" Result", result)

Illustration Call a state- changing function

transaction_hash= contract.functions.set (42). Distribute

({' from'" 0xsenderAddress",' gas' 100000})

Print (" sale Hash", transaction_hash)

6. Harkening to Events

• You can also hear to events emitted by the smart contract. Define an event listener function and use the contract. Events affiliate to subscribe to events.

Def event-listener (event)

Print (f" Event entered-{event (' event')} {event ('

args')}")

Subscribe to an event

event_filter= contract.events.MyEvent.create sludge

(fromBlock = "rearmost")

event_filter=Watch (event_listener)

<u>Exploring Different styles of Interaction</u>

1. Original Ethereum Node (Ganache)

• Set up an original Ethereum knot using tools like Ganache for development and testing. Connect your Python script to this original knot for quick and effective commerce during the development phase.

2. Infura or Alchemy for Remote Nodes

• Use remote Ethereum bumps handed by services like Infura or Alchemy for connecting to the Ethereum mainnet or testnets. This is useful when you do not want to run an original knot or need access to a specific Ethereum network.

3. Etherscan APIs

• Etherscan provides APIs that allow you to interact with the Ethereum blockchain without running a knot. These APIs can be used for querying balances, costing sale details, and interacting with smart contracts.

4. Metamask Wallet

• Metamask is a popular Ethereum portmanteau and cybersurfer extension that allows druggies to interact with DApps. It provides a JavaScript library that inventors can integrate into their web operations to enable flawless stoner relations with smart contracts.

5. Web3.py for Ethereum Classic (ETC)

•Web3.py can also be used for interacting with Ethereum Classic. Simply connect to an Ethereum Classic knot, emplace the contract, and interact with it in an analogous fashion as with Ethereum.

6. Using Python Smart Contract Libraries

• Libraries like eth- abi and eth- contract give fresh tools for working with Ethereum smart contracts in Python. They can simplify certain aspects of contract commerce and data garbling.

7. Blockchain Explorer APIs

• Blockchain explorers like Etherscan offer APIs that give information about deals, blocks, and smart contracts. These APIs can be useful for covering and costing data from the Ethereum blockchain.

- For testing smart contracts, tools like Pytest and Brownie can be employed. Brownie, in particular, is a Python-grounded development and testing frame for Ethereum smart contracts that streamlines the testing process.

Interacting with smart contracts involves choosing the applicable system grounded on your development terrain, whether it's an original knot, a remote knot, or third- party services.

By using Python and libraries likeWeb3.py, inventors can fluently integrate smart contract functionality into their operations and scripts, enabling a flawless connection between decentralized operations and the Ethereum blockchain.

TESTING AND DEBUGGING SMART CONTRACTS

Icing the security and functionality of smart contracts is pivotal before deployment to the blockchain.

Testing and debugging are integral corridor of the development process to identify and fix implicit vulnerabilities and bugs.

In this environment, we'll explore strategies for testing smart contracts and debugging ways for Python- grounded smart contracts. Strategies for Testing Smart Contracts

1. **Automated Testing**

• Unit Tests Write unit tests to corroborate the correctness of individual functions within the smart contract. Libraries like Truffle for Ethereum or Brownie for Python give testing fabrics for writing automated tests.

• Integration Tests Test the relations between different factors and contracts. Insure that the entire system behaves as anticipated when multiple contracts work together.

• Functional Tests produce tests that pretend real-world scripts to validate the functionality of the smart contract in colorful situations.

2. **Use Testnets**

• Emplace and test your smart contract on test networks (testnets) like Ropsten or Rinkeby before planting to the mainnet. This helps identify any issues related to the factual deployment terrain.

3. Code Review

• Conduct thorough law reviews with peers or external adjudicators. Multiple perspectives can help identify implicit security vulnerabilities or advancements in law effectiveness.

4. Stationary Analysis Tools

• Employ static analysis tools that dissect the law without executing it. Tools like MythX and Slither can identify common security issues and implicit vulnerabilities in your smart contract law.

5. Fuzz Testing

• Use fuzz testing ways to induce arbitrary inputs and deals to identify unanticipated actions and vulnerabilities. Fuzz testing tools like Echidna for Ethereum can be precious for this purpose.

6. Gas Estimation

• Estimate gas consumption during contract prosecution to insure that deals are doable within the Ethereum network's gas limits. High gas consumption can lead to sale failures.

7. Edge Case Testing

• Test your smart contract with extreme and edge- case scripts to corroborate how it behaves under unusual conditions. This includes testing with maximum and minimal values, as well as other boundary conditions.

Debugging ways for Python- grounded Smart Contracts

1. Logging

• Introduce logging statements in your Python- grounded smart contract law to track the inflow of prosecution and affair variable values. Reviewing logs can help pinpoint the position of implicit issues.

Illustration Logging

Contract SimpleStorage

Def set (tone, x)

Print (f" Setting value to{x}")

Tone. Stored data = x

2. Publish Statements

• Use print statements to affair values and remedy information during prosecution.

This is a simple yet effective way to understand the state of variables and the control inflow.

3. **Testnet Debugging**

• Emplace and test your Python- grounded smart contract on a testnet using a development terrain like Brownie. This allows you to interact with the contract and observe its geste in a controlled terrain.

4. Parrots and Simulators

• Use blockchain parrots or simulators that replicate the geste of the Ethereum blockchain. This allows you to test and remedy your smart contract locally without interacting with the factual blockchain.

5. Tracing Tools

• Use tools that give sale tracing capabilities. These tools record the prosecution way of your smart contract, making it easier to identify the source of crimes.

6. Remedying with Remix

• Remix is a web- grounded IDE that supports the debugging of Ethereum smart contracts. It allows you to emplace and remedy your Python- grounded smart contracts using the erected- in debugger.

7. Event Logging:

• Emit events in your smart contract law to log important state changes or conduct. You can also subscribe to these events and dissect them to understand the geste of the contract during prosecution.

Debugging smart contracts requires a combination of ways, including automated testing, homemade testing, and interactive debugging. By espousing a methodical approach to testing and using available tools, inventors can insure the robustness and security of their smart contracts before planting them to the blockchain.

Also, staying informed about best practices and security considerations is pivotal in the fleetly evolving geography of blockchain development.

PLANTING PYTHON-SPOKEN SMART CONTRACTS ON ETHEREUM

Planting smart contracts on the Ethereum blockchain involves several way, including collecting the contract law, preparing the deployment sale, and configuring gas freights and network parameters.

In this environment, we'll explore how to emplace Python- written smart contracts on Ethereum using a development terrain like Brownie.

Using elf for Deployment Brownie is a popular development and testing frame for Ethereum smart contracts, written in Python.

It simplifies the deployment process and provides an important interface for interacting with Ethereum smart contracts.

1. Installation

• Install elf using pip pip install eth- elf produce a

2. Brownie Project

• Initialize a new Brownie design using the following command

Bash Copy law   elf init

3. Write Your Smart Contract

• Write your smart contract law in Python. Save it in the contracts directory.

Then is a simple illustration

Python Copy

Law SimpleStorage.sol

Pragma reliability0.8.0;   contract

Simple Storage {uint256 storedData;

Function set (uint256 x)

Public {storedData = x;   function get () public view

returns (uint256) {return storedData;

4. Configure Deployment Script

• produce a deployment script (e.g., deploy.py) in the scripts directory. This script will be responsible for planting the smart contract.

Python Copy law

deploy.py

From elf import SimpleStorage, accounts, network

Def main ()

Emplace the smart contract

simple_storage= SimpleStorage.deploy ({' from' accounts (0)}) Interact with the smart contract. Set (42, {' from' accounts (0)}) stored_value = simple_storage. Get ({' from' accounts (0)}) print (f" Stored value {stored_value}")

5. Configure Network Parameters

• Edit the elf-config.yaml train to configure network parameters. Specify the network you want to emplace to and the gas price you're willing to pay.

Yaml Copy law

Networks   dereliction development

gas_price: auto

• For deployment to the Ethereum mainnet or testnets, you will need to give your Ethereum account private key or use a portmanteau provider like MetaMask for authentication.

6. Emplace the Smart Contract

• Run the deployment script using the elf press

Bash Copy law

Elf runscripts/deploy.py-- network

• Replace with the asked Ethereum network (e.g., mainnet, rinkeby, ropsten, or development for an original testnet).

Configuring Gas freights and Network Parameters

1. Gas freights

• Gas freights are paid for every operation on the Ethereum network. The gas price determines the cost of each unit of gas. You can configure gas freights in the elf-config.yaml train under the asked network.

Yaml Copy law

Networks

Dereliction development

Development bus

• Setgas_price to bus to stoutly determine the gas price grounded on the network conditions. Alternately, set it to a specific value in Gwei.

2. Gas Limit

• The gas limit represents the maximum quantum of gas you're willing to spend on a transaction. However, the sale will fail, if the contract prosecution exceeds this limit.

You can specify the gas limit in the deployment script

Python Copy law

simple_storage =SimpleStorage.deploy ({' from' accounts (0),'gas_limit' 500000})

3. Network Configuration

• Configure the network parameters in the **'elf-config.yaml train'**. For deployment to the Ethereum mainnet or testnets, you need to give your Ethereum account private key.

Yaml Copy law

Networks:

Default: development

Development:

gas_price: auto

Mainnet:

gas_price: auto

Unlock:

- "your_private_key"

Rinkeby:

gas_price: auto

Unlock:

- "your_private_key"

• Ensure that you handle private keys securely and don't expose them in public depositories.

Flash back to exercise caution when dealing with private keys and planting contracts on the Ethereum mainnet. Always follow security stylish practices and consider using tackle holdalls

Or portmanteau providers for secure crucial operation. Also, completely test your smart contracts on testnets before planting them to the mainnet.

DECENTRALIZED OPERATIONS (DAPPS)

Preface to DApps

Decentralized operations (DApps) are an order of operations that operate on blockchain networks, offering the benefits of decentralization, translucency, and invariability.

Unlike traditional operations, DApps aren't controlled by a single reality, and their sense is generally executed by smart contracts on a blockchain.

Crucial Characteristics of DApps

1. Decentralization

• DApps run on decentralized networks, generally grounded on blockchain technology. This means that there's no single point of control or failure, making them resistant to suppression.

2. Translucency

• All deals and conduct within a DApp are recorded on the blockchain, furnishing translucency and auditability. Druggies can corroborate the integrity of the operation's sense and data.

3. Invariability

• Once stationed on the blockchain, the law and data of a DApp are inflexible. Changes to the operation bear agreement from the network, icing a tamper- evidence terrain.

4. Open Source:

• Numerous DApps are open- source, allowing anyone to check the law, contribute advancements, and inspection the security of the operation.

5. Cryptographic Security:

• DApps use cryptographic ways for stoner authentication, data integrity, and secure deals. Private keys give druggies with control over their means and relations with the operation.

6. Tokenization

• DApps frequently involve the use of commemoratives, which can represent power of means, advancing rights, or other functionalities within the operation.

7. Smart Contracts

• DApps generally calculate on smart contracts, tone- executing law on the blockchain that enforces the rules and sense of the operation. Smart contracts enable unsure relations between parties.

Structure DApps with Python and Smart Contracts

Structure a DApp involves creating both the frontal end (stoner interface) and the aft end (smart contracts on the blockchain). Below is a simplified companion on erecting a DApp using Python and smart contracts on the Ethereum blockchain.

1. Smart Contract Development

• Write the smart contract law in a language like reliability. Save the contract law in a train with a. sol extension.

Solidity Copy code

// SimpleStorage.sol

Pragma solidity ^0.8.0;

Contract SimpleStorage {

Uint256 storedData;

Function set (uint256 x) public {

StoredData = x;

}

Function get () public view returns (uint256) {

Return storedData;

}

}

2. Collect the Smart Contract

• Use a reliability compiler (e.g., solc) to collect the smart contract law into bytecode and ABI (operation double Interface).

Bash Copy law

SolcSimpleStorage.sol-- caddy-- abi-- optimize- o. / affair

3. Emplace the Smart Contract

• Use a deployment script to emplace the smart contract to the Ethereum blockchain. A tool like Brownie simplifies this process. Write a deployment script in Python.

Python Copy law

deploy.py

From elf import SimpleStorage, accounts

Def main ()

Emplace the smart contract = SimpleStorage.deploy ({' from' accounts (0)})

Print (f" Contract stationed at {simple_storage. address}")

• Run the deployment script using the elf press.

Bash Copy law

Elf runscripts/deploy.py-- network

• Make a simple web interface for your DApp using a Python web frame like Flask. Produce HTML templates and use Flask to serve them.

Python Copy code

```python
# app.py
From flask import Flask, render_template
From brownie import SimpleStorage, accounts


App = Flask (__name__)
simple_storage = SimpleStorage.deploy ({'from':
accounts [0]})


@app.route ('/')
Def home ():
Return render_template ('index.html',
value=simple_storage.get ())


If __name__ == '__main__':
app.run (debug=True)
```

5. HTML Template (index.html):

• Produce an HTML template for the DApp's frontend. Use JavaScript to interact with the smart contract.

In the next page …..

```html
<! -- index.html -->
<! DOCTYPE html>
<html Lang="en">
<Head>
<Meta charset="UTF-8">
<Meta name="viewport" content="width=device-
width, initial-scale=1.0">
<Title>SimpleStorage DApp</title>
</head>
<Body>
<h1>SimpleStorage DApp</h1>
<p>Stored Value: <span id="value"> {{value}}
</span></p>
<button onclick="setValue ()">Set Value</button>


<Script>
Async function setValue () {
Const newValue = prompt ('Enter new value :');
If (! isNaN (newValue)) {
```

```
Const accounts = await ethereum.request
({method: 'eth_requestAccounts'});
Const contract = new ethers.Contract
('ContractAddress', ['function set (uint256)'], new
ethers.providers.Web3Provider
(web3.currentProvider).getSigner ());
Await contract.set (newValue);
location.reload ();
} else {
Alert ('Invalid input. Please enter a number.');
}
}
</script>
</body>
</html>
```

• Change 'ContractAddress' to the smart contract's deployed address.

<u>**Start the Flask application:**</u>

• To observe the DApp in operation, launch the Flask app.

Python app.py

• Open a web cybersurfer and visit http// localhost5000 to interact with your Python-written DApp.

This is an introductory illustration, and real-world DApps involve more sophisticated features, security considerations, and considerations for stoner experience.

When erecting DApps, it's pivotal to consider gas freights, stoner authentication, secure crucial operation, and adherence to stylish practices for smart contract development. The choice of blockchain platform, libraries, and tools will also depend on the specific conditions of the DApp.

ORACLES AND DATA FEEDS IN SMART CONTRACTS

Preface Smart contracts on blockchain networks are tone- executing and deterministic, meaning they calculate on the data available on the blockchain. Still, numerous real- world scripts bear information from external sources, similar as price feeds, rainfall data, or sports scores. Oracles serve as islands between smart contracts and these external data sources, furnishing a medium to bring out- chain data onto the blockchain.

Oracles for External Data Integration

1. Description

• A mystic is a trusted reality that fetches and verifies real- world data and also relays it to a smart contract. Oracles play a pivotal part in decentralized operations by allowing smart contracts to interact with external information.

2. Types of Oracles

• **Software Oracles:** These oracles are enforced as software running on a centralized garçon. They cost data from colorful sources and submit it to the blockchain.

• **tackle Oracles:** these oracles calculate on external tackle bias, similar as IoT detectors, to give data to the smart contract.

• **Consensus Oracles:** multiple oracles give data, and an agreement medium is used to determine the accurate information. This approach enhances security and reduces the threat of manipulation.

3. Integrating Oracles in Smart Contracts

• **Oracle Contracts:** Smart contracts can emplace mystic contracts to grease communication with external sources. These contracts act as interposers, costing and vindicating data before passing it to the main smart contract.

• **API Calls:** Some oracles grease data integration by making API calls to external sources. The mystic queries the external API, verifies the data, and provides it to the smart contract.

• **Decentralized Oracle Networks:** These networks involve multiple bumps (oracles) that inclusively give data. By achieving agreement, decentralized mystic networks enhance security and trust ability.

Handling Data Feeds Securely

1. Data Source Verification

- insure that the data source furnishing information to the mystic is estimable and secure. Vindicating the authenticity of the data source is pivotal for precluding vicious data injection.

2. Consensus Mechanisms

- Use agreement mechanisms within the mystic network to corroborate the delicacy of the data. Consensus ensures that data handed to the smart contract is agreed upon by multiple independent oracles.

3. Data Aggregation

- Aggregate data from multiple sources to enhance delicacy and reduce the impact of potentially incorrect data from a single source.

This approach is particularly effective in decentralized mystic networks.

4. **Security checkups**

• Conduct security checkups of both the smart contract and the mystic result. Independent checkups by estimable security enterprises can help identify vulnerabilities and insure the overall robustness of the system.

5. **Secure Communication**

• Use secure communication channels between the mystic and external data sources. Encryption and secure protocols (HTTPS, TLS) help cover against data tampering during transmission.

6. **Timestamping**

• Timestamp the data at the source and record it on the blockchain. This helps establish a clear chronological order for data entries, precluding manipulation by furnishing an inflexible record.

7. Fail- safe-deposit box Mechanisms

• apply fail-safe mechanisms in the smart contract to handle unanticipated situations, similar as attainability of the mystic or invalid data. These mechanisms can include fallbacks, time- outs, or indispensable data sources.

8. Profitable impulses

• Design profitable impulses for oracles to bear actually. Price mechanisms and penalties can encourage oracles to give accurate data and discourage vicious geste

9. Upgradeability

• Consider making the mystic result upgradeable to acclimatize to changing conditions and security norms. This allows for advancements and adaptations without compromising the integrity of the system.

10. Decentralization

• Choose decentralized mystic results and networks to alleviate single points of failure. Decentralization enhances adaptability and reduces the threat of data manipulation.

11. Stoner Authentication

• If applicable, apply stoner authentication mechanisms to insure that only authorized druggies or realities can query or interact with the mystic and the associated smart contract.

By precisely enforcing and securing oracles, inventors can extend the capabilities of smart contracts to incorporate real- world data, making blockchain operations more protean and important. Security, trustability, and decentralization are crucial considerations when integrating oracles and handling data feeds in smart contracts.

TOKENIZATION AND TOKEN NORMS CREATING COMMEMORATIVES USING PYTHON

Tokenization involves representing real or digital means on a blockchain as commemoratives. These commemoratives can represent power, access rights, or other means, and they can be transferred and traded on blockchain networks. Then is a simplified illustration of creating commemoratives using Python on the Ethereum blockchain using the Brownie frame.

1. **Install elf**

• Install the elf frame, a development and testing terrain for Ethereum smart contracts.

Bash Copy code

Pip install eth-brownie

2. **Create a New Brownie Project:**

• Launch a fresh Brownie project.

Bash Copy code

Brownie init

3. **Write the Token Smart Contract:**

• Make a new Solidity file (Token.sol, for example) and provide the smart contract for the token.

Solidity Copy code

```solidity
// Token.sol
Pragma solidity ^0.8.0;


Contract SimpleToken {
Mapping (address => uint256) public balances;


Event Transfer (address indexed from, address indexed
to, uint256 value);


Function mint (address to, uint256 value) public {
Balances [to] += value;
Emit Transfer (address (0), to, value);
}


Function transfer (address to, uint256 value) public {
Require (balances [msg.sender] >= value,
"Insufficient balance");
Balances [msg.sender] -= value;
Balances [to] += value;
```

Emit Transfer (msg.sender, to, value);

}

}

4. Deploy the Token Smart Contract:

• To deploy the token smart contract, write a deployment script (deploy.py, for example).

Python Copy code

 # deploy.py

From brownie import SimpleToken, accounts

Def main ():

 # Deploy the token smart contract

Token = SimpleToken.deploy ({'from': accounts [0]})

Print (f"Token deployed at: {token.address}")

• Use the Brownie console to execute the deployment script.

Bash Copy code

5. Interact with the Token Smart Contract:

- To mint and transfer tokens, write a basic interaction script (interact.py, for example).

Python Copy code

```python
# interact.py
From brownie import SimpleToken, accounts


Def main ():
# Connect to the deployed token smart contract
Token = SimpleToken.at ("ContractAddress") #
Replace with the actual contract address


# Mint tokens to an account
token.mint (accounts [1], 1000)


# Transfer tokens between accounts
token.transfer (accounts [2], 500)


# Print balances
Print (f"Balance of Account 1: {token.balances
(accounts [1])}")
Print (f"Balance of Account 2: {token.balances
(accounts [2])}")
```

- • Use the Brownie console to execute the interaction script.

Brownie run scripts/interact.py --network development

This is an introductory illustration, and real-world token contracts would include fresh features similar as allowance, events, and potentially more complex sense. Also, the below illustration uses the development network; for deployment to the Ethereum mainnet or testnets, fresh configurations and considerations are demanded.

Overview of Token norms

Token norms are specifications that define how commemoratives should be enforced on a blockchain.

These norms insure comity and interoperability between different commemoratives and platforms.

There are two extensively used token norms on the Ethereum blockchain

1. ERC- 20(Ethereum Request for commentary 20)

• ERC- 20 is the most common commemorative standard on the Ethereum blockchain. It defines a set of rules and functions that commemoratives must follow to be considered ERC- 20 biddable. Crucial features include • **Balance Tracking:** The standard specifies how balances are tracked and how transfers can be made.

Approval Mechanism: Allows token holders to delegate spending rights to other addresses.

• Events Defines events similar as **Transfer** to track token movements.

- Example ERC- 20 functions **totalSupply**, **balanceOf**, **transfer**, **authorize transferFrom**.

2. ERC- 721(Ethereum Request for commentary 721)

- ERC- 721 introduces the conception of non-fungible commemoratives (NFTs), each with a unique identifier. Unlike ERC- 20 commemoratives, each ERC- 721 commemorative is distinct and can represent power of unique means. Crucial features include:

• Power Commemoratives are possessed by a specific address and can only be transferred by the proprietor.

• **Metadata:** Supports fresh metadata for each commemorative, making each token unique.

• **Interfaces:** Specifies functions for checking power, getting token information, and transferring power.

• Example ERC- 721 functions **balance of**, **proprietor of**, **safe Transfer From**, **token URI**.

Inventors choose the applicable commemorative standard grounded on the use case. ERC- 20 is suitable for commutable commemoratives (e.g., mileage commemoratives), while ERC- 721 is ideal for representing power of unique means (e.g., digital collectibles, in- game means).

When creating commemoratives, it's essential to cleave to these norms to insure comity with being platforms and tools.

GOVERNANCE AND DAOS (DECENTRALIZED AUTONOMOUS ASSOCIATIONS)

Enforcing Governance Mechanisms in Smart Contracts

Governance mechanisms in smart contracts allow decentralized decision- making by token holders or members of a community. These mechanisms can include voting on proffers, making opinions about protocol upgrades, and managing finances. Then are crucial factors to consider when enforcing governance in smart contracts:

1. **Token- grounded Voting**

• Tie advancing power to power of commemoratives. Token holders can cast votes proportionate to their token effects. This ensures a fair and decentralized decision- making process.

2. **Voting proffers**

• Proffers are conduct or opinions that token holders can bounce on. Proffers can include protocol upgrades, fund allocation, or changes to governance rules. Proffers are submitted to the community for blessing.

3. **Quorum and Thresholds**

• Define quorum and voting thresholds for proffers to be accepted. Quorum represents the minimal participation needed for a vote to be valid, while the threshold is the minimal chance of blessing demanded for an offer to pass.

4. Timelocks

• apply timelocks on proffers to help hurried or vicious decision- timber. Timelocks insure that proffers are open for advancing for a specified period before results are perfected.

5. Dynamic Governance Rules

• Allow for flexible governance rules that can be acclimated grounded on the evolving requirements of the community. For illustration, the community might decide to change the voting quorum or threshold through a governance offer.

6. Exigency arrestment

• Include an exigency arrestment medium that allows the community to halt operations in the event of a critical issue or security vulnerability. This provides a fresh subcaste of protection.

7. **Governance Token Upgrades**

- Plan for upgrades to the governance commemorative itself. This could involve token migrations or upgrades to the smart contract to add new governance features or ameliorate being bones

8. **Translucency and Auditability**

    - insure translucency in governance by furnishing clear information on proffers, advancing results, and token effects. Periodic checkups by third- party security enterprises can enhance the credibility of the governance system.

Structure DAOs with Python

Building a Decentralized Autonomous Organization (DAO) involves creating a smart contract that governs the association's decision-making processes. Below is a simplified illustration using Python and the Brownie Framework?

1. **Install elf**

• Install the elf frame if not formerly installed.

Pip install eth-brownie

2. **Create a New Brownie Project:**

• Launch a fresh Brownie project.

Brownie init

3. **Write the DAO Smart Contract:**

• Create the DAO smart contract in a Solidity file (such as DAO.sol).

// DAO.sol

Pragma solidity ^0.8.0;

Contract DAO {

Mapping (address => uint256) public votingPower;

Mapping (address => bool) public hasVoted;

Event ProposalSubmitted (address indexed proposer, uint256 indexed proposalId);

Event VoteCasted (address indexed voter, uint256 indexed proposalId, bool support);

Struct Proposal {

Address proposer;

String description;

Uint256 forVotes;

Uint256 againstVotes;

Bool executed;

}

Proposal [] public proposals;

Uint256 public proposalCount;

Function submitProposal (string memory _description) public {

Require (votingPower [msg.sender] > 0, "Only members can submit proposals");

proposals.push (Proposal ({

Proposer: msg.sender,

Description: _description,

ForVotes: 0,

AgainstVotes: 0,

Executed: false

}));

ProposalCount++;

Emit ProposalSubmitted (msg.sender,

proposalCount);

}

Function castVote (uint256 _proposalId, bool

_support) public {

Require (! hasVoted [msg.sender], "You have

already voted");

Require (_proposalId > 0 && _proposalId <=

proposalCount, "Invalid proposal ID");

Proposal storage proposal = proposals

[_proposalId - 1];

If (_support) {

proposal.forVotes += votingPower [msg.sender];

} else {

proposal.againstVotes += votingPower

[msg.sender];

}

HasVoted [msg.sender] = true;

Emit VoteCasted (msg.sender, _proposalId,

_support);

}

}

4. **To implement the DAO smart contract,**

Create a deployment script (deploy.py, for example).

Python Copy code

 # deploy.py

From brownie import DAO, accounts

Def main ():

 # Deploy the DAO smart contract

Dao = DAO.deploy ({'from': accounts [0]})

Print (f"DAO deployed at: {dao.address}")

- Use the Brownie console to execute the deployment script.

Bash Copy code

Brownie run scripts/deploy.py --network development

5. **To communicate with the DAO Smart Contract,**

Create an interaction script (such as interact.py) and use it to make suggestions and cast votes.

Python Copy code

```python
# interact.py
From brownie import DAO, accounts

Def main ():
    # Connect to the deployed DAO smart contract
    Dao = DAO.at ("ContractAddress") # Replace with the actual contract address

    # Submit a proposal
    dao.submitProposal ("Upgrade the protocol")

    # Cast votes on proposals
    dao.castVote (1, True)
    dao.castVote (1, False)
```

- Use the Brownie console to execute the interaction script.

Bash Copy code

This illustration represents an introductory DAO with offer submission and voting functionality. A completely functional DAO would include fresh features similar as quorum conditions, timelocks, and offer prosecution sense. Also, security considerations, checkups, and testing are pivotal when enforcing governance mechanisms in smart contracts and erecting DAOs.

SCALING RESULTS FOR SMART CONTRACTS

Scalability is a critical challenge in the blockchain space, especially for smart contracts. As blockchain networks grow, the number of deals and the computational cargo on smart contracts increase, leading to implicit backups. Several results have been proposed and enforced to address these scalability challenges.

Two prominent approaches are Subcaste 2 results and sidechains.

Challenges in Smart Contract Scalability

1. High sale Costs

• On popular blockchains like Ethereum, sale costs, generally known as gas freights, can be high during ages of network traffic. This makes it expensive for druggies to interact with smart contracts.

2. Network Traffic

• As the number of druggies and deals increases, blockchain networks can witness traffic, performing in slower evidence times for deals.

3. Limited Outturn

• Numerous blockchains have limited sale outturn, meaning they can only reuse a certain number of deals per second. This limitation hinders the scalability of smart contracts.

4. Storehouse and prosecution Costs

- Storing and executing smart contracts bear computational coffers. As the complexity and size of smart contracts increase, so do the associated costs.

5. Scalability Trilemma

- The scalability trilemma suggests that it's challenging to achieve a balance between scalability, security, and decentralization. Perfecting one aspect frequently comes at the expenditure of the others.

Exploring Scaling results

1. Subcaste 2 Scaling

- Description

- Subcaste 2 results involve erecting fresh structure" on top" of the being blockchain to discharge some deals from the main chain, thereby perfecting scalability.

• **State Channels**: Actors produce private channels for out- chain deals, and only the final state is settled on the main chain.

• **Tube:** utilizes a scale of sidechains (child chains) that periodically submit summaries of their state to the main chain (root chain).

• **Rollups:** summations deals off- chain and posts a single evidence to the main chain, reducing on- chain computational costs.

• Faster sale evidence times.

• Reduced sale costs for out- chain relations.

• Alleviates traffic on the main chain.

• Challenges

• icing security and trustlessness of out- chain deals.

• Designing effective exit mechanisms in case of controversies.

• Coordinating communication between different layers.

2. <u>Sidechains</u>

• Description

• Sidechains are separate blockchains connected to the main blockchain, allowing means and data to be transferred between them. They give a way to gauge smart contract prosecution singly.   •

Types

• **Federated Sidechains:** Governed by a group of trusted realities.

- **Drivechain Sidechains:** Use intermingled mining to partake security with the main chain.

- **Mongrel Side chains:** Combine rudiments of both allied and drivechain sidechains.

- **Benefits**

- Increased outturn by parallelizing deals on sidechains.

- Customizable agreement mechanisms.

- Inflexibility in designing specific features for different use cases. • **Challenges**

- icing security and precluding implicit attacks.

- Managing interoperability between the main chain and sidechains. • Achieving decentralization while maintaining performance advancements.

3. <u>Sharding</u>

• Description

• Sharding involves partitioning the blockchain into lower, connected parts called shards. Each shard processes a subset of deals, enabling resemblant processing and perfecting scalability.

• Benefits

• Increased outturn by recycling deals in parallel.

• Lower sale freights and faster evidence times.

• Enhanced overall network scalability.

• Challenges

• icing secure communication and collaboration between shards. • Designing effective cross-shard communication mechanisms.

• Managing state thickness across shards.

4. <u>Auspicious Rollups</u>

• **Description**

• Auspicious Rollups are a type of Subcaste 2 scaling result that optimistically processes deals off- chain and posts a summary (rollup) on- chain. Controversies are resolved on- chain only if necessary.

• **Benefits**

• Significant reduction in on- chain calculation and costs.

• Faster futurity for deals.

- Enhanced scalability without compromising security.

• **Challenges**

• Handling controversies and icing effective resolution.

• Balancing the trade- off between on- chain and off- chain processing.

• icing stoner-friendly gests during the disagreement resolution process.

These scaling results aim to address the challenges associated with smart contract scalability, offering different trade- offs between decentralization, security, and performance.

The ongoing development and perpetration of these results contribute to the elaboration of the blockchain ecosystem, making it more suitable for different use cases and mass relinquishment.

SEQUESTRATION AND CONFIDENTIALITY IN SMART CONTRACTS

Icing sequestration and confidentiality in smart contracts is pivotal, as blockchain deals are generally transparent and visible to all actors on the network.

Achieving sequestration involves securing sensitive information and sale details from being penetrated or viewed by unauthorized parties.

There are crucial considerations for enhancing sequestration in blockchain deals and enforcing nonpublic smart contracts icing

Sequestration in Blockchain Deals

1. Public vs. Private Blockchains

- **Public Blockchains:** Deals on public blockchains, similar as Bitcoin and Ethereum, are visible to all actors. Sequestration is achieved through pseudonymity, where portmanteau addresses aren't directly tied to real- world individualities.

- **Private Blockchains:** Private Blockchains circumscribe access to a predefined set of actors. While these offer further control over sequestration, they immolate decentralization compared to public blockchains.

2. Zero- Knowledge Attestations (ZKPs)

• ZKPs allow one party to prove the validity of a statement without revealing any information about the statement itself. This enables private deals and calculations on a public blockchain. ZKPs include protocols like zk- SNARKs (zero- knowledge brief non-interactive arguments of knowledge) and zk- STARKs (zero- knowledge scalable transparent arguments of knowledge).

3. Ring Autographs

• Ring autographs enable sequestration by obscuring the true sender in a group of implicit signers. Monero, a sequestration- concentrated cryptocurrency, uses ring autographs to insure sender obscurity.

4. Nonpublic Deals

• Nonpublic deals hide the sale amounts on the blockchain. Rather of displaying exact values, they use cryptographic commitments to insure that the sum of inputs equals the sum of labors without revealing individual quantities.

5. Homomorphic Encryption

• Homomorphic encryption allows calculations to be performed on translated data without decoding it. This can be applied to private smart contracts where data remains nonpublic during processing.

6. Sidechains and Off- Chain Deals

• Sidechains or off- chain results enable deals to do down from the main blockchain, reducing visibility. Ways like state channels, payment channels, and sidechain agreements contribute to sequestration advancements.

7. Blockchain Mixing Services

• Mixing services or trapezists allow druggies to combine their deals with those of other actors, making it delicate to trace the source and destination of finances. Still, the effectiveness of mixing services may vary.

8. **Enforcing Identity results**

• Decentralized identity results, similar as tone-autonomous identity (SSI), enable druggies to have control over their identity information. This can ameliorate sequestration by allowing druggies to partake only the necessary information in an empirical manner.

Enforcing Confidential Smart Contracts with Python

Implementing nonpublic smart contracts frequently involves using sequestration-concentrated technologies and fabrics. Then is a simplified illustration using the PySyft library, which integrates with PyTorch to apply sequestration- conserving machine literacy models.

1. **Install PySyft**

• Install the PySyft library.

Bash Copy code

Pip install syft

2. **Confidential Smart Contract Example:**

• Create a simple confidential smart contract using PySyft for privacy-preserving computations.

Python Copy code

```python
# confidential_contract.py
Import syft as sy
Import torch

Hook = sy.TorchHook (torch)

# Create two private tensors
Alice = sy.VirtualWorker (hook, id="alice")
x = torch.tensor ([5, 10]).private (owners="alice")

Bob = sy.VirtualWorker (hook, id="bob")
y = torch.tensor ([2, 3]).private (owners="bob")

# Perform a private computation
z = x + y

# Retrieve the result
Result = z.get ()
Print (result)
```

3. Execute the Confidential Smart Contract:

• Launch the script for the confidential smart contract.

Python confidential_contract.py

• The result of the private calculation will be published, and actors (Alice and Bob) can keep their input tensors private.

This illustration uses PySyft to perform private calculations on private tensors possessed by different virtual workers (representing different actors).

Note that this is an introductory illustration, and enforcing more complex nonpublic smart contracts involves considerations for security, sequestration guarantees, and the specific use case conditions. Sequestration and confidentiality in smart contracts are evolving areas with ongoing exploration and development. The choice of sequestration-enhancing technologies and fabrics depends on the specific requirements and constraints

of the use case.

SMART CONTRACT AUDITING

<u>**Significance of Auditing Smart Contracts**</u>

Auditing smart contracts is a pivotal step in the development and deployment process to insure the security, trust ability, and functionality of the law. Smart contracts, being tone- executing and inflexible pieces of law on the blockchain, bear thorough checkups to identify and address implicit vulnerabilities.

The significance of auditing smart contracts includes

1. Security Assurance

• Checkups help identify and alleviate security vulnerabilities, icing that smart contracts are resistant to attacks, exploits, and vicious conditioning.

2. Guarding stoner finances

• Smart contracts frequently handle fiscal deals and manage precious means. A security breach could affect in the loss of stoner finances. Auditing helps help similar incidents.

3. Code Quality and Best Practices

• Checkups insure that smart contracts cleave to stylish coding practices, optimizing for readability, effectiveness, and maintainability. This helps help unintentional bugs and crimes.

4. Regulatory Compliance

• In some cases, smart contracts need to misbehave with legal and nonsupervisory norms. Auditing can help identify implicit issues and insure compliance with applicable regulations.

5. Trust and Reputation

• A well- checked smart contract inspires trust among druggies, inventors, and the broader community. It enhances the design's character and credibility.

6. Precluding Exploits and Attacks

• Auditing helps identify common vulnerabilities similar as reentrancy attacks, overflow/ underflow issues, and other vulnerabilities that could be exploited by bushwhackers.

7. Ensuring Business Logic

• Checkups corroborate that the smart contract's business sense aligns with the intended functionality and that it directly reflects the terms of the associated decentralized operation (DApp).

Auditing Tools and Stylish Practices

1. Manual Code Review

• Endured blockchain inventors and adjudicators manually review the smart contract law line by line, relating implicit issues and icing adherence to stylish practices.

2. Automated Scanners

• Tools like MythX, Slither, and Oyente can automatically overlook smart contract law for common vulnerabilities and implicit security pitfalls. These tools round homemade checkups by snappily relating implicit issues.

3. Stationary Analysis

• Stationary analysis tools dissect the law without executing it, relating implicit vulnerabilities, and furnishing perceptivity into law structure and dependences.

4. Dynamic Analysis

• Dynamic analysis involves executing the smart contract in a controlled terrain to identify runtime vulnerabilities. Tools like Manticore and Echidna perform dynamic analysis.

5. Fuzz Testing

• Fuzz testing involves subjugating the smart contract to a large number of arbitrary inputs to identify unanticipated geste, vulnerabilities, or edge cases.

6. Gas Analysis

• assaying gas consumption is pivotal for optimizing smart contract performance and relating implicit vulnerabilities related to gas limits and costs.

7. Security norms Compliance

• Insure that the smart contract adheres to security norms similar as the ConsenSys Best Practices and the OpenZeppelin library, which give guidelines for secure smart contract development.

8. Attestation Review

• Review the attestation to insure that it directly reflects the willed geste of the smart contract. Deficient or inaccurate attestation can lead to misconstructions and vulnerabilities.

9. Nonstop Monitoring

• Apply nonstop monitoring tools and practices to descry and respond to implicit security issues indeed after the smart contract is stationed.

10. Third- Party checkups

- Engage third- party security enterprises or adjudicators with moxie in smart contract security to give an independent and thorough assessment.

11. Public Bug Bounty Programs

- Encourage the community to share in bug bounty programs. Offering rewards for relating and responsibly telling vulnerabilities can attract professed security experimenters.

12. Community Review

- Encourage the design's community to review and give feedback on the smart contract law. A different set of eyes can contribute precious perceptivity.

Smart contract auditing is an iterative process, and it's essential to incorporate security considerations throughout the entire development lifecycle.

A combination of homemade reviews, automated tools, and community engagement contributes to a comprehensive and effective smart contract inspection. Regular updates and checkups are pivotal as the blockchain geography evolves, and new vulnerabilities and stylish practices crop.

CROSS-CHAIN DEVELOPMENT WITH PYTHON

Building Smart Contracts that Interact with Multiple Blockchains

Cross-chain development involves structure smart contracts that can interact with multiple blockchains. This capability is precious for creating decentralized operations (DApps) and smart contracts that bear interoperability across different blockchain networks. Then are crucial considerations and way forcross-chain development using Python

1. **Choose a Cross-Chain Development**

    Framework:

• Elect across-chain development frame or library that supports interoperability between different blockchains. Exemplifications include Polkadot, Cosmos, and Interledger.

2. **Use Cross-Chain Smart Contract norms:**

• Use cross-chain smart contract norms that enable communication and relations between blockchains. Exemplifications include the Interledger Protocol (ILP) for payment channels and the ERC- 20 and ERC- 721 norms for token interoperability on Ethereum.

3. **Ground Contracts:**

• Apply ground contracts that act as interposers between different blockchains. These contracts lock means on one blockchain and mint original means on another, enabling flawless transfer and representation of value.

4. Oracle Integration:

• Integrate oracles to cost and bear information between blockchains. Oracles give external data to smart contracts, enabling them to make informed opinions grounded on real- world events or conditions.

5. Cross-Chain Messaging:

• Develop a messaging subcaste that facilitates communication between smart contracts on different blockchains. This subcaste can use standard messaging protocols to insure comity.

6. Interoperable Token norms:

• Utensil token norms that are interoperable across different blockchains. This ensures that commemoratives can be transferred and employed seamlessly between networks.

7. Cross-Chain Identity and Authentication:

• Develop identity and authentication mechanisms that work across multiple blockchains. This is pivotal for icing harmonious and secure stoner gests across different decentralized operations.

8. Infinitesimal barters:

• Explore infinitesimal exchange technologies that allow druggies to change means across different blockchains without the need for interposers. Infinitesimal barters insure that either the entire sale occurs or none of it does.

9. Smart Contract Portability:

• Design smart contracts with portability in mind. Consider factors similar as contract state, data formats, and prosecution surroundings to insure that contracts can operate on different blockchains without revision.

Cross-Chain Interoperability Considerations

1. **Consensus Mechanisms:**

• Different blockchains may use varying agreement mechanisms. Consider how the agreement mechanisms of connected blockchains may impact the security and futurity of cross-chain deals.

2. **Sale Futurity**

• Understand the futurity mechanisms of connected blockchains. Some blockchains may have faster futurity than others, impacting the speed and certainty of cross-chain deals.

3. Security

• estimate the security models of the blockchains involved. Consider implicit attack vectors and insure thatcross-chain deals maintain a high position of security.

4. Scalability

• Assess the scalability of connected blockchains, as scalability issues on one chain may impact the performance of cross-chain deals.

5. Interoperability norms

• Cleave to established interoperability norms to insure that smart contracts and commemoratives can seamlessly move between blockchains. This enhances comity and usability.

• Consider how governance and upgrade mechanisms on one blockchain may affect connected blockchains. Insure that changes in one blockchain don't negatively impact the interoperability of the entire ecosystem.

7. Attestation and norms Compliance

• Give clear attestation for inventors using your cross-chain smart contracts. Insure compliance with norms to grease wide relinquishment and integration into different operations.

8. Cross-Chain Testing

• Conduct expansive testing of cross-chain functionalities, considering colorful scripts and implicit edge cases. This includes testing for security vulnerabilities, unanticipated actions, and performance issues.

9. Stoner Experience

• Prioritize a flawless stoner experience for individualities interacting with cross-chain DApps. Druggies should be suitable to distribute across different blockchains with minimum disunion.

10. Legal and Regulatory Considerations

• Understand and misbehave with legal and nonsupervisory conditions across different authorities where the connected blockchains operate. Compliance is pivotal for the long-term success and sustainability of cross-chain systems.

Cross-chain development with Python requires a solid understanding of blockchain generalities, smart contract development, and the specifics of the connected blockchains.

As the blockchain ecosystem evolves, inventors are likely to see further tools and libraries that grease cross-chain interoperability, making it easier to make decentralized operations that gauge multiple blockchains.

LEGAL AND NONSUPERVISORY CONSIDERATIONS IN SMART CONTRACT DEVELOPMENT

Overview of Legal Aspects in Smart Contract Development

Smart contracts, being tone- executing pieces of law, introduce unique legal considerations. Inventors and associations engaging in smart contract development should be apprehensive of the legal counteraccusations and navigate the complex geography of regulations. Here's an overview of crucial legal aspects in smart contract development:

1. Contract Validity

• Smart contracts are subject to traditional contract law principles. It's important to insure that the terms and conditions decoded in the smart contract are fairly enforceable and cleave to contract conformation conditions.

2. Law as Law

• the conception of" law as law" implies that the law itself dictates the terms and conditions of a smart contract. Still, legal systems may intermediate in cases of fraud, misrepresentation, or other illegal conditioning, emphasizing that law isn't a cover for legal principles.

3. Regulatory Compliance

• Smart contracts may need to misbehave with colorful nonsupervisory fabrics depending on their purpose and the authorities in which they operate. Compliance with securities, consumer protection, data sequestration, and anti-money laundering regulations is pivotal.

4. Digital Autographs

• Digital autographs play a pivotal part in smart contracts. Understanding the legal validity and recognition of digital autographs in different authorities is essential for icing the enforceability of agreements.

5. Liability and Responsibility

• Determining liability and responsibility in the event of a smart contract malfunction or unintended outgrowth is a complex legal issue.

Legal fabrics may need to evolve to address liability enterprises associated with automated and decentralized systems.

6. Consumer Protection

• If smart contracts involve consumer deals, they may be subject to consumer protection laws. Icing translucency, fairness, and adherence to consumer rights is essential to avoid legal challenges.

7. Intellectual Property

• Smart contract inventors should consider intellectual property rights, similar as brand and patent law, especially if the law contains innovative or personal rudiments. Open- source licensing and clear attestation can address intellectual property enterprises.

8. Data sequestration

• Smart contracts frequently involve the processing of particular data. Compliance with data protection laws, similar as GDPR in the European Union, is critical. Enforcing sequestration- conserving measures within smart contracts is a crucial consideration.

Compliance and Regulatory Considerations

1. Know your client (KYC) andAnti-Money Laundering (AML) Compliance

• If a smart contract involves fiscal deals, inventors must consider KYC and AML regulations. Enforcing identity verification measures and complying with reporting conditions are essential.

2. Securities Regulations

• Smart contracts involving token deals or crowd funding may be subject to securities regulations. Compliance with these regulations, including enrollment conditions and investor protection measures, is pivotal.

3. Token Bracket

• Commemoratives issued through smart contracts may be classified as securities, mileage commemoratives, or other orders. Different nonsupervisory conditions apply grounded on the bracket. Consulting with legal experts is advised to insure compliance.

4. Jurisdictional Considerations

• The legal status of smart contracts can vary across authorities. Developers should be apprehensive of the legal fabrics in the authorities where the smart contract will be stationed and used.

5. Smart Contract Audits

• Conducting regular security checkups on smart contracts isn't just a stylish practice for law quality but can also contribute to compliance. Relating and addressing security vulnerabilities can help legal issues stemming from contract breaches.

6. Regulatory Reporting

• Smart contracts that handle fiscal deals or sensitive data may be needed to misbehave with reporting scores. Understanding and fulfilling these reporting conditions is essential for legal compliance.

- Establish mechanisms for disagreement resolution in the smart contract. This could involve incorporating traditional legal disagreement resolution processes or exploring decentralized arbitration and agreement options.

8. Legal Attestation

- Easily validate the legal aspects of the smart contract in accompanying attestation. Terms of use, disclaimers, and other legal vittles should be fluently accessible to druggies.

9. Regular Legal Updates

• Given the evolving nature of blockchain and smart contract regulations, it's important to stay informed about legal developments. Regularly streamlining smart contracts to align with changing legal conditions is essential.

10. Legal Consultation

• Seek legal advice from experts specializing in blockchain and smart contract law. Legal professionals can give perceptivity into compliance conditions, implicit legal pitfalls, and strategies for mollifying legal challenges.

Navigating the legal geography in smart contract development requires a multidisciplinary approach involving legal professionals, inventors, and compliance experts. Staying informed about nonsupervisory developments and proactively addressing legal considerations is pivotal for the successful and fairly sound deployment of smart contracts.

SMART CONTRACT UPGRADABILITY

Smart contract upgradability is a critical consideration in blockchain development, allowing inventors to apply advancements, fix bugs, and acclimatize to changing conditions without dismembering being druggies or operations. Achieving upgradability involves careful design and the perpetration of ways that enable the flawless elaboration of smart contracts over time.

Ways for elevation Smart Contracts

1. Proxy Contracts

• Proxy contracts act as interposers between druggies and the factual perpetration contracts. The deputy contract delegates calls to the current perpetration contract. When an upgrade is demanded, a new perpetration contract is stationed, and the deputy is streamlined to point to the new perpetration.

This allows for flawless upgrades without changing the contract's address.

2. Eternal storehouse

• Separate the data storehouse enterprises from the contract's sense by using an eternal storehouse contract.

The sense contract references the storehouse contract, and when an upgrade is demanded, a new sense contract is stationed while maintaining the same storehouse contract. This preserves the state and allows for sense updates.

3. Upgradeable Libraries

• Use upgradeable libraries for common functionalities that may need frequent updates. Libraries are stationed independently, and contracts can source these libraries. When a library needs an update, a new interpretation is stationed, and contracts are upgraded to use the rearmost interpretation.

4. Delegate Call

• Employ the delegate Call opcode, which allows a contract to execute law from another contract's environment. This can be used for in- place upgrades by planting a new contract with streamlined sense and having the being contract delegate calls to the new bone. This is a more gas-effective way of achieving upgradability.

5. Governance Mechanisms

• Apply governance mechanisms that allow a decentralized community or set of crucial stakeholders to inclusively decide on upgrades. This can involve multi-signature wallet, token-holder voting, or other agreement mechanisms to authorize and legislate upgrades.

6. Time- Locked Upgrades

• Introduce time- locked upgrades, where a new interpretation of the contract is stationed but activation is delayed until a specified time has passed or certain conditions are met. This provides a grace period for druggies to review and raise enterprises before the upgrade takes effect.

<u>Icing backward comity</u>

1. Formalized Interfaces

• Use formalized interfaces similar as ERC- 20 or ERC- 721 to define the functions and actions of smart contracts. When upgrading, insure that the new contract adheres to the same interface to maintain comity with being operations and services.

2. Fallback Functions

• save fallback functions and event structures in the upgraded contract. Being operations and services may calculate on specific actions, and maintaining these fallback functions helps insure backward comity.

3. Deprecation Notices

• give clear deprecation notices in the attestation and within the smart contract itself. Notify druggies about forthcoming upgrades, disapproved functions, and changes in geste. This helps druggies acclimatize to the changes and modernize their relations consequently.

4. Versioning

• Include versioning mechanisms in your smart contract design. This could involve bedding interpretation information in contract state variables or events. Druggies and operations can also check the interpretation before interacting with the contract to acclimatize to any changes.

5. Community Engagement

• Engage with the community and druggies throughout the upgrade process. Seek feedback, address enterprises, and involve the community in decision- making regarding upgrades. A transparent and cooperative approach helps maintain trust and stoner confidence.

6. Testnets and Carrying surroundings

• Test upgrades completely on testnets and carrying surroundings before planting them on the mainnet. This allows inventors to identify and address implicit issues, icing a smooth transition for druggies.

7. Conclude- In Upgrades

• Whenever possible, make upgrades conclude- in for druggies. Allow them to resettle to the new interpretation at their convenience rather than forcing immediate relinquishment. This approach gives druggies more control over when and how they transition to the upgraded contract.

8. Fallback Mechanisms

• Utensil fallback mechanisms or graceful declination in case of unanticipated issues. This ensures that, indeed if an upgrade encounters unlooked-for challenges, the contract can still serve with minimum dislocation until issues are resolved. Smart contract upgradability is a delicate balance between maintaining a secure and stable system and allowing for inflexibility and elaboration.

By employing careful planning, transparent communication, and backward-compatible design principles, inventors can successfully navigate the challenges of smart contract upgrades while icing a positive experience for druggies and stakeholders.

REAL- WORLD USE CASES OF PYTHON IN BLOCKCHAIN

Python is a protean programming language that has set up substantial relinquishment in the blockchain space due to its readability, inflexibility, and expansive ecosystem of libraries and fabrics. Then are some real- world use cases and case studies of successful systems where Python has been employed in blockchain development:

1. Ethereum Smart Contracts and DApps

• Use Case Ethereum, one of the leading blockchain platforms, relies heavily on Python for smart contract development. Libraries likeWeb3.py grease commerce with the Ethereum blockchain, and fabrics like Brownie streamline smart contract testing and deployment.

2. DeFi Protocols and Platforms

• Use Case multitudinous decentralized finance (DeFi) systems and platforms use Python for their backend structure and smart contract development. exemplifications include advancing protocols like Aave and decentralized exchanges(DEXs) like Uniswap, where Python is employed for colorful factors, including automated request makers(AMMs), liquidity provision, and smart contract relations.

3. Blockchain Analytics and Data Services

• Use Case Python is extensively used in blockchain analytics platforms similar as Chainalysis and Coin Metrics. These platforms influence Python's data analysis and visualization libraries to give perceptivity into blockchain deals, identify patterns, and enhance nonsupervisory compliance.

4. Supply Chain and Provenance

• Use Case Companies like IBM Food Trust use Python for developing smart contracts and operations that enhance force chain translucency and traceability. Python's ease of integration with other technologies and its data processing capabilities make it suitable for handling complex force chain data.

5. Identity operation and Authentication

• Use Case Self-autonomous identity results, similar as Sovrin, use Python for developing decentralized identity systems. Python's support for cryptography and its use in erecting secure systems make it suitable for identity operation on the blockchain.

6. Tokenization Platforms

• Use Case Python is employed in tokenization platforms that enable the creation and operation of digital means on the blockchain. Platforms like Polymath use Python for smart contract development, allocation, and operation of security commemoratives.

7. Healthcare Data Management

• Use Case systems like Medical chain use Python for developing smart contracts and operations that secure and manage healthcare data on the blockchain. Python's robustness and support for data processing contribute to maintaining the integrity and sequestration of sensitive health information.

8. Decentralized Autonomous Associations (DAOs)

• Use Case DAOs, which are associations governed by smart contracts, frequently use Python for their development. Aragon, a platform for erecting DAOs, provides libraries and tools in Python for creating and managing decentralized governance structures.

9. Energy Trading Platforms

• Use Case Python is employed in blockchain-grounded energy trading platforms, where druggies can buy and vend renewable energy directly.

Systems like Power Ledger influence Python for smart contract development and backend systems that grease peer- to- peer energy trading.

10.Gaming and Non-Fungible Commemoratives

(NFTs)

• Use Case Python is used in the development of blockchain- grounded gaming platforms and NFT commerce. CryptoKitties, a popular NFT game, utilizes Python for colorful backend functionalities, including smart contract relations and stoner interfaces.

These real- world use cases demonstrate the different operations of Python in blockchain development across different diligence. Python's versatility, combined with its active inventor community and rich ecosystem, makes it a favored language for erecting decentralized operations, smart contracts, and blockchain-related tools.

SMART CONTRACT STANDARDIZATION AND PATTERNS

1. Homogenizing Smart Contract Development Practices

Homogenizing smart contract development practices is essential for creating interoperable and secure contracts that cleave to common norms. This helps inventors, adjudicators, and druggies understand and interact with smart contracts more effectively. Some crucial areas of standardization include

i. Interface norms

- Define clear and standardized interfaces for contracts, especially for functionalities like token norms (e.g., ERC- 20, ERC- 721) to insure comity across colorful operations and platforms.

ii.   Attestation

• Give comprehensive attestation for smart contracts, detailing their functionality, styles, events, and any other applicable information. Clear attestation enhances translucency and facilitates easier integration.

iii.   Event Logging

• regularize event logging to make it easier for external operations to hear and respond to events emitted by smart contracts. Well- defined events enhance the contract's usability and interoperability.

iv.   Error Handling

• Establish harmonious error handling mechanisms, including error dispatches and error canons, to ameliorate the stoner experience and aid inventors in troubleshooting.

v.   Security Best Practices

• Apply security stylish practices, similar as avoiding the use of disapproved functions, icing input confirmation, and following secure coding norms to alleviate common vulnerabilities.

vi.   Gas Optimization

• Optimize gas operation by employing effective coding ways, avoiding gratuitous calculations, and optimizing storehouse operations. Gas-effective contracts are more cost-effective for druggies.

vii.   Upgradability norms

• If the contract is designed to be upgradeable, follow standardized upgrade patterns to insure smooth transitions between different contract performances without compromising security or dismembering functionality.

viii. Testing norms

• Borrow standardized testing fabrics and procedures, including unit testing, integration testing, and security testing, to insure the trust ability and robustness of smart contracts.

2. <u>Design Patterns for Applicable and Effective law:</u>

Design patterns in smart contract development give applicable results to common problems and promote law effectiveness, maintainability, and security. Then are some extensively used design patterns

i.   **Plant Pattern**

• The plant pattern involves creating a separate contract responsible for planting and managing cases of another contract. This pattern is useful for managing multiple cases of analogous contracts.

ii.   **Proxy Pattern**

• The Proxy pattern involves using a deputy contract to delegate calls to an underpinning perpetration contract. This allows for upgradability without changing the contract's address.

iii.   **State Machine Pattern**

• apply a state machine to represent the different countries a contract can be in and control transitions between countries. This pattern is useful for contracts with complex workflows.

iv.   Withdrawal Pattern

• Use the Withdrawal pattern to handle fund recessions securely. This pattern separates the sense for fund transfers, reducing the threat of reentrancy attacks.

v.   Commit- Reveal Pattern

• The Commit- Reveal pattern is frequently used in gaming or voting operations. It involves a two-step process where actors first commit to a choice, and latterly reveal their commitment. This prevents frontal- handling attacks.

vi.   Oracle Pattern

• When external data is needed, use the Oracle pattern to cost data securely. This involves using a mystic contract to act as a trusted source of information.

vii.   **Circuit Breaker Pattern**

• Apply a circuit swell to pause or disable certain functionalities in the contract in case of extremities or unanticipated geste. This pattern enhances the contract's security and allows for timely intervention.

viii.   **Observer Pattern**

• The Observer pattern involves emitting events that external contracts or operations can hear to. This enables effective communication between smart contracts and external systems.

ix.   **Part- Grounded Access Control (RBAC) Pattern**

• apply RBAC to manage warrants and access control within a smart contract. This pattern is precious for contracts with multiple places and liabilities.

### x.	Upgradeability Patterns

• Colorful patterns, similar as the Eternal storehouse pattern, can be employed to achieve upgradability without compromising the integrity of the contract's state.

By espousing standardized practices and using design patterns, smart contract inventors can enhance law quality, reduce the liability of crimes, and promote thickness in the development process.

These approaches contribute to a more secure and interoperable blockchain ecosystem.

SMART CONTRACT MONITORING AND ANALYTICS

Monitoring and assaying the performance of smart contracts are critical aspects of maintaining a healthy and secure blockchain ecosystem. By enforcing effective monitoring tools and analytics, inventors can gain perceptivity into contract geste, identify implicit issues, and optimize contract performance. There are some aspects to consider

1. **Tools for Monitoring Smart Contract Performance:**

a. **Tracers and Debuggers**

• Example Tools EtherScan, Tenderly, Ethers.js

• These tools allow inventors to trace and remedy deals, examining each step of contract prosecution. They give visibility into function calls, gas operation, and state changes, abetting in the identification of implicit issues.

b. Gas Analyzers

• Example Tools GasTracker, GasNow

• Gas analyzers help track and dissect gas consumption by smart contracts. This is pivotal for optimizing contract effectiveness, minimizing sale costs, and relating implicit gas- related issues.

c. Security Auditing Tools

• Example Tools MythX, Securify, Slither

• Security auditing tools dissect smart contract law for implicit vulnerabilities and security pitfalls. They help inventors identify and address security issues before deployment, reducing the threat of exploits.

d. Network Explorer Tools

• Example Tools EtherScan, Blockchair, BlockCypher

• Network explorers give real- time information about deals, blocks, and contract relations on the blockchain. They're precious for covering the overall health of the blockchain network and shadowing specific smart contract conditioning.

e. Profilers

• Example Tools Solidity Gas Profiler

• Profilers help inventors dissect the gas consumption of individual functions within a smart contract. Profiling can identify backups and areas for optimization, contributing to more effective contract prosecution.

• Example Tools Grafana, Prometheus

• Real- time monitoring platforms allow inventors to produce customized dashboards for covering smart contract criteria. These tools can integrate with colorful data sources to give comprehensive perceptivity into contract performance.

2. <u>Enforcing Analytics in Python</u>

a. **Web3.py Library**

•Web3.py is a Python library for interacting with Ethereum- suchlike blockchains. It allows inventors to query blockchain data, recoup sale details, and cover events emitted by smart contracts. Python scripts can be written usingWeb3.py to dissect contract relations.

Python Copy code

From web3 import Web3

# Connect to a local Ethereum node
w3 = Web3 (Web3.HTTPProvider ('http:
//localhost:8545'))

Get contract events
contract_address =
'0x123456789abcdef123456789abcdef123456789a'
contract_abi = [...] # ABI of the smart contract
Contract = w3.eth.contract (address=contract_address,
abi=contract_abi)

# Retrieve events
Events = contract.events. My Event ().get Logs
(fromBlock=0, to Block='latest')

analyze events data
For event in events:

 # analyze event data here

Print (event)

b. Python Data Analysis Libraries

• Libraries similar as Pandas, NumPy, and Matplotlib can be used for in- depth data analysis of smart contract relations. These libraries give tools for data manipulation, statistical analysis, and visualization.

Python Copy code

Import pandas as Pd

 # Create a Data Frame from contract event data

DF = pd.Data Frame (events)

 # analyze and visualize data

Print (df.head ())

df.plot(x='timestamp', y='value', kind='line')

c. Grafana and Prometheus Integration

• Grafana and Prometheus can be integrated into a Python- grounded analytics channel. Python scripts can cost and reuse smart contract data, and Grafana dashboards can fantasize the results.

d. Machine Learning for Anomaly Detection

• Python's machine literacy libraries, similar as scikit- learn and Tensor Flow, can be applied to dissect smart contract data for anomalies or unusual patterns. This can help descry implicit security pitfalls or abnormal geste.

From sklearn.ensemble import Isolation Forest

 # Example anomaly detection with scikit-learn

Model = Isolation Forest (contamination=0.05)

DF ['anomaly_score'] = model.fit_predict (DF [['value']])

Print (DF [DF ['anomaly_score'] == -1])

Enforcing analytics in Python allows inventors to work the rich ecosystem of data analysis tools and libraries. Whether it's covering gas operation, assaying sale patterns, or relating security vulnerabilities, Python provides a flexible and important terrain for smart contract analytics.

FUTURE TRENDS IN PYTHON AND BLOCKCHAIN

The blockchain space is dynamic, and several arising technologies and trends are shaping its future. Python, with its versatility and wide relinquishment, continues to play a pivotal part in the development and elaboration of blockchain operations. Then are some crucial trends and considerations for the unborn

1. <u>Integration of Python with Web3 Libraries</u>

   • As blockchain ecosystems evolve, the integration of Python with Web3 libraries (similar asWeb3.py for Ethereum) will continue to enhance the development experience. Python's simplicity and readability make it a favored language for structure operations that interact with blockchain networks.

2. Cross-Chain Development

•Cross-chain development, allowing smart contracts to interact seamlessly across multiple blockchain networks, is gaining traction. Python, with its expansive ecosystem, may see increased relinquishment in systems that concentrate on interoperability, allowing inventors to make decentralized operations that gauge different blockchains.

3. Decentralized Finance (DeFi) Innovation

• The rapid-fire growth of DeFi systems is likely to continue, with Python being a prominent language for developing fiscal operations. Python's robust libraries for data analysis and machine literacy may also contribute to threat assessment and analytics within DeFi protocols.

4. Non-Fungible Commemoratives (NFTs) and Python

• Python is anticipated to play a part in the development of NFT platforms and commerce. As NFTs extend beyond digital art to colorful diligence, Python's versatility may be abused to produce, manage, and trade unique digital means on the blockchain.

5. Sequestration and Confidentiality results

• Sequestration- concentrated blockchain results and nonpublic smart contracts are getting more current. Python may be employed in developing sequestration- conserving technologies and protocols, icing secure and nonpublic deals on the blockchain.

6. Scalability results

• Addressing scalability challenges remains a precedence in the blockchain space.

Python's part in enforcing and optimizing subcaste 2 scaling results, side chains, and sharding ways could come more prominent as the assiduity explores ways to enhance sale outturn.

7. Smart Contract Auditing and Security

• With an increased emphasis on security, Python is likely to play a pivotal part in smart contract auditing and security analysis. Tools and fabrics for stationary analysis, dynamic analysis, and formal verification of smart contracts may continue to be developed in Python.

8. <u>Governance Mechanisms and DAOs</u>

• Decentralized Autonomous Associations (DAOs) are anticipated to come more sophisticated, and Python could be involved in the development of governance mechanisms. Python's readability may contribute to the transparent and accessible perpetration of governance rules and processes.

9. <u>Green and Sustainable Blockchain</u>

<u>Development</u>

• Sustainability enterprises are getting more prominent in the blockchain space. Python may play a part in the development of energy-effective agreement mechanisms and sustainable blockchain results, aligning with the growing focus on environmental considerations.

10. <u>Regulatory Compliance results</u>

As the nonsupervisory geography for blockchain becomes clearer, Python may be used to apply tools and fabrics that grease nonsupervisory compliance within blockchain operations. This could include identity verification, KYC processes, and compliance reporting.

11. <u>Continued Growth of Blockchain Platforms Supporting Python-</u>

The integration of Python into colorful blockchain platforms is likely to continue. Blockchain systems and protocols that support Python-grounded smart contract development, similar as Ethereum, Binance Smart Chain, and others, will contribute to Python's sustained applicability in the blockchain ecosystem.

12. <u>Education and Training enterprise</u>

With the adding demand for blockchain inventors, education and training enterprise concentrated on Python and blockchain development are anticipated to grow. Online courses, tutorials, and coffers will

Probably feed to inventors looking to enter the blockchain space using Python.

In summary, Python is poised to remain a crucial player in the blockchain ecosystem, with ongoing benefactions to colorful aspects of blockchain development.

As the assiduity matures, Python's rigidity, readability, and expansive library support position it well for addressing the evolving challenges and openings in the blockchain space.

CONCLUSION

In this disquisition of Python- grounded blockchain development, we covered crucial generalities, use cases, and trends in the crossroad of Python programming and blockchain technology. Then is a recap of the crucial generalities bandied

1. <u>Python in Blockchain</u>

<u>Development</u>

• Python's readability, versatility, and expansive ecosystem make it a popular choice for blockchain development.

• Libraries similar asWeb3.py grease commerce with blockchain networks, and fabrics like Brownie simplify smart contract development.

2. Book Ideas on Python Programming

• Explored book ideas covering a range of Python programming motifs, including data wisdom, web development, machine literacy, and blockchain.

3. Table of Contents for" Python for Blockchain Development Building Smart Contracts"

• Outlined a comprehensive table of contents for an academic book, covering colorful aspects of Python- grounded blockchain development.

4. Smart Contract Development

• Explored crucial areas in smart contract development, including Python basics, reliability, security, testing, deployment, and commerce with decentralized operations (DApps).

5. <u>Smart Contract Upgradability</u>

• bandied ways for upgrading smart contracts and icing backward comity, allowing for the elaboration of contracts over time.

6. <u>Legal and Regulatory</u>

<u>Considerations</u>

• Explored legal and nonsupervisory aspects in smart contract development, emphasizing compliance, data sequestration, intellectual property, and the significance of legal discussion.

7. <u>Smart Contract Monitoring and</u>

<u>Analytics</u>

• bandied tools for covering smart contract performance and enforcing analytics in Python, enabling inventors to gain perceptivity and optimize contract geste.

8. Unborn Trends in Python and Blockchain

• Examined arising trends, including cross-chain development, DeFi invention, NFTs, sequestration results, scalability, smart contract auditing, governance mechanisms, sustainability, and continued growth of Python- supported blockchain platforms.

Next Steps

Still, there are some recommended coming way if you are interested in farther literacy and disquisition in Python- grounded blockchain development.

1. **Explore Blockchain Platforms**

• Gain hands- on experience by exploring popular blockchain platforms that support Python- grounded smart contract development, similar as Ethereum, Binance Smart Chain, and others.

2. **Online Courses and Tutorials**

• Enroll in online courses and tutorials that concentrate on Python and blockchain development. Platforms like Coursera, Udacity, and Codecademy offer courses acclimatized to different skill situations.

3. **Read Attestation and Source law**

• Dive into the attestation of blockchain platforms and libraries. Explore the source law of being Python- grounded blockchain systems on GitHub to understand stylish practices and perpetration details.

4. Community Engagement

• Join online communities and forums related to Python and blockchain development. Engage with other inventors, ask questions, and share in conversations to enhance your understanding and network with professionals in the field.

5. Contribute to Open Source systems

• Contribute to open- source blockchain systems written in Python. This not only allows you to apply your knowledge but also provides precious experience and exposure to cooperative development practices.

6. Trial with Smart Contract Deployment

• Set up a development terrain and trial with planting smart contracts. Produce simple contracts, interact with them, and gain practical experience in the deployment and prosecution of smart contracts.

7. Stay Informed about Trends

• Stay streamlined on the rearmost trends and developments in Python and blockchain. Follow estimable blogs, attend conferences, and share in webinars to stay informed about arising technologies and stylish practices.

8. Build Real- World systems

• Apply your knowledge by working on real-world systems. This could involve developing your decentralized operation, contributing to a being design, or creating tools that enhance the blockchain development workflow.

Flash back, blockchain technology is continually evolving, and staying curious and visionary in your literacy trip will contribute to your success as a Python- grounded blockchain inventor.

Whether you are interested in decentralized finance, NFTs, or other blockchain operations, the combination of Python and blockchain offers instigative openings for invention and disquisition.